The Only World I Knew

a collection of poems

Meg Barratt

The Only World I Knew

Published 2010

Published by Noel Barratt

Printed by
Steers Printing,
140 Railway Terrace,
Rugby,
CV21 3HN

ISBN 978-0-9567225-0-8

Forward

"My career as a ballroom dancer was cut off in its prime by the Jehovah's Witnesses", or at least that's how Meg always said that her autobiography would start. The tale of how the cinema, together with its upstairs room where Meg took ball room dancing lessons, was turned into the local Kingdom Hall, was one that she never converted into poetry, but much of her childhood she did.

When Meg died we felt ourselves to be immensely lucky to have the treasury of her poems to remember her by. Poems that left us in no doubt as to who she loved, what she remembered, and what she thought important. There are poems here that will evoke strong memories for those who grew up in post war Britain. There are poems that will speak to those who share Meg's love of the natural environment. There are poems about people Meg knew and people she didn't, poems in which you might recognize parts of yourself. There are poems that have made us laugh, and poems that have made us cry. All of them we wanted to share by publishing them together in this collection.

You will find some notes after the poems which help to put some into context, others need no such comment.

We hope you enjoy this book and, as you read the poems, have the feeling that they speak to and for you.

Noel, Ruth and Kate.

A Nose For The Past

Stately home, or no, as I went down
the well-worn winding steps
I was back in the cellar at Gran's,
scent of damp and dolly-blue,
white-wash, maybe, but not the coal
nor the shaft of sunlight from the grid
as the black cobs rumbled gleaming down,
leaving choking dust motes in the air.
Here were hanging tucked, lace gowns,
petticoats and pantaloons for display,
not the worn tea-towels drooping limply
over my head with rough, striped shirts
for drying on the wooden rack,
artistically arranged laundry tools
instead of Grandad's treasure hoard
of biscuit tins full of nuts and bolts
screws and washers, nameless bits,
ancient toys and the wind-up gram
I claimed to be my own.
This room had forgotten such things,
or never known them, but the walls
remembered pungently the smell.

Stranger

The back room's home at number twenty four,
Coal fire burning low in sooty grate,
Black iron kettle steaming on the hob,
Polished fender, socks on rail of brass,
Old rag rug, rust table cloth chenille,
Straight backed chairs for Gran and Grandad, Mum and me.

A shocking khaki stranger calls my name,
Sharp cap, stiff greatcoat, boots and trunk,
Horror cushions my face in deep familiar chair
Worn-out, washed-out shades of patchwork pink,
The scent of Grandad's Woodbine lingers round my head,
Its smoke wisps hanging in the shattered air.
Six clocks tick steady, mark this potent moment,
Each in their own time and in mine.
The feathers cannot dull the fearful sense
I am the only stranger present here.

Saturday Silence

Saturday evening, waiting for the draws
From the rhythmic chant of the lighted wooden box,
Breath and voice bated by Wall's Neapolitan,
The striped complete family block,
While he made noughts and crosses patterns
Intently, on the mystery sheet,
With sucks and sighs,
Words soundlessly forbidden.

Similar silence was for horses
Bet on down in Pollitt's yard, with Gran's
Six penn'orth each way on Piggot,
Shoulders signing the result,
Ritual counting of next week's ration
Of mint-green packets from the cardboard case
To keep the atmosphere cloudy and contribute
To thrombosis, that cost a leg first
And then a life.

Precision demanded quiet when
The drawers within drawers of clock parts,
Mental and physical, were frowningly fitted
To tick around the walls.
Patience cards turned after each other,
Jigsaw pieces flipped to strip colour,
Only shape and pattern matter here at all.

Two wars had rejected him, too small,
Turned him out a bitter little man,
Did not listen to the one inside who
Finished school full of pride,
Knowing 'all they could teach'.
He turned to fixing things, gramophones, clocks,
To selling records, sweets and cigs,
To the brass factory turning wheels and cogs,
The poker leaning in my hearth,
Jumping on the work bench from a standing start
To be noticed, 'swearing like a trooper',
So they said, and yet at Gran's we never
Heard a misplaced word.

Theme Song

Did Henry know, do you imagine,
when he wrote that tune?
Did he think its great effect would be
to charm some elegant lady of the court
in her latest finery, green sleeves and all?
The charm's still working like the Piper's flute,
drawing children from house and garden,
t.v. and play-station, to seek out the van,
eagerly answer its call.

True other chimes sound out to ring the changes,
like the 'Stop me and buy one' bicycle bell,
but none is so enduring, not Twinkle, Twinkle,
nor The Teddy Bear's Picnic of childhood,
tinny notes speaking of longed for cornet,
one lickable scoop, on special occasions two,
chocolate sauce or raspberry juice trickling
to make a gruesome spectacle of the hand,
tub, dripping wafer, ninety-nine,
and Next-door with a basin, counting
a snowball scoop per person for the family.

Less spontaneous, haphazard now,
advertised orderliness and hygiene rule the day,
but still the tinkling theme has its magnetic pull.
Oh Henry! Dream of your composition
and let drop an icy tear.

Bush Fires 2009

I'm bemused by the sheer beauty of Hell,
the glorious gold-red flame consuming
trees, grass, homes, everything
in its whirling, unpredictable path,
leaving dark, twisted skeletons,
elaborate patterns of white and black
and a small, fur-coated creature,
nuzzling puzzled against its rescuer's cheek.

The photos are acutely clear,
explicit images captured
by a fire-fighter, I'm told.
But it wasn't the pictures
that really brought it home,
no, not those, but the one line
in the e-mail explaining,
'We couldn't breathe for the smoke
billowing in our road'.

Instantly my back was leaning
against our warm front wall, watching,
but even more, smelling
the prefab opposite blazing.
That pungent stench, unlike
campfire, bonfire, fire in the grate,
invariably carries me back
to that fearful, childhood conflagration.
Recalling this now, I'm thrust
into the terror of wild bush fires in Victoria.

Peace-Fire

We sat in the top of the flat pan-cake tree
Polly-Pauline and me, just where the trunk
Split for her den and mine, and we
Thought noble thoughts of our great good fortune
To live in the country ...the club playing fields
Slow brook, bushes, the banks both slutchy
Plank to bramble-strewn remnants of gardens
On to the tip and forbidden Mersey.

Now was the time for serious planning
No means for slash and burn we must
Drag what we could from field and hedge
Beg broken chairs, bust doors and other junk
Cram papers on the bogey with an old tin trunk
Bundle anything burnable into Polly's pram
Ferry the loot to the flat wash-house roofs
For safety from other marauding groups
Set guards till bed-time under the lamp
And wait for the great day.

We'd build the fire out in the road,
No need to worry about cars
No cars round our drive then
No-one posh enough for that
Mr. Mason's Mayflower hadn't moved for years
Probably never would. Our traffic was
The rumbling metal roller-skate hurtling
The scooter pushed at break-knee pace
The bikes and trikes for ever circling,
Grooving the pavement,
Or small kid racers harnessed as horses
In the non-skipping season.

The stack is built and folk come drifting out
Somebody's dad helps hoist a doubtful guy
Onto a table-throne banger-powered
Drooping as flames shoot round his booted feet
And rip-raps burst round ours.
There's rockets and sparklers, candles and fountains
Catherine-wheels, cannons and pink-smoking mountains
Someone brings sausages rolled in sliced bread
Someone's dark toffee pulls teeth from our heads
As we watch the blaze sink lower.

Polly-Pauline nudges me, 'Look at that!'
As she points out two shapes disturbing the embers
It's the Johnson and Rafter mums close to the heat
Last week they were fighting out here in the street
'Our Tony, your Ian', that sort of thing
And now they're stood chatting, part of the ring
Swigging beer, poking 'taters out from the ash
To look you would think there was never a clash
And neither bashed the other.

We've got to go in though we'd rather stay later,
'Just till I've finished one last baked potato'
'I'll see you tomorrow down by the tree'
We've plenty to talk about Polly and me
Minds inspired by woodsmoke we very plainly saw
If everyone had bonfires we could put an end to war.

Michael

A barrier of blue split our prefabs
Blue blue irises, low enough to jump
Dodging Michael's grandad's watering can.
Oh we were good at dodging that's for sure
Making our escape to dangers all our own
'Bet you daren't jump the brook, there's rats in there'
Slipping deep into rhododendron dens,
Swinging, riding the whirling witch's hat
Too cowardly-brave to own how sick we felt
Falling in nettles in the ditch the worst
That ever could befall a pair like us.

They told me all about it, I heard words,
Running to his Gran, a road, a shout, a car
And Michael dead, they said.
I knew what 'dead' was, birds and spiders, frogs
That was sad but what I felt now was not sad
I stared into flowers, what could they mean,
A barrier of puzzled blue
Between my wondering self and them.

Seaside

Too cold to do more than dip a toe,
that gently lapping sea
but the child without fail prepares to go
ready to plunge into white waves
on water the colour of cold weak tea.

Cornwall freezing, the Hebrides mild,
it made no sense at all.
Over the ripples and lug worm castes, piled
firm in the arch of her foot,
she races in answer to the sea's call.

A slimy line of seaweed so she jumps,
a scallop makes her pause,
and mooching round some tempting flotsam lumps,
she shivers at the stranded jellyfish
surrounded by a crab's abandoned claws.

Reaching the waves at the bright sea's brink,
she splashes, shrieking loud
and feeling itchy wool begin to sink,
clutches soggy swimsuit to goose-pimpled chest,
relieved there is no nosey staring crowd.

Swing

Swing out, swing in
Swing hung on the coal shed door
Soar out, jerk back in
Out again for more

Standing on the back yard step
Twenty bantams eyeing me
Every one with hostile peck,
Lav beyond the fierce brown sea,
Cower in fear for threatened legs
But I really need a wee.

Rush out, dash back in
Safe behind the door.

Through the door to join the class
Twenty new girls' eyes all stare
Scorning last term's summer dress
Past the neat brown ranks, my chair,
Smile, determined, none-the-less
I will not be welcome there.

Swing out, swing in
Swing hung on the coal shed door
Jerk in, soar back out
Out again for more.

The Reader

Shuffle-marching from the hall,
Harry Lime Theme for a treat,
Light in squares shines on the table
As I squeeze into my seat,
'Dick see Dora, Nip see Fluff',
Oh, I'm weary of this stuff.

Staring through bars of windows,
Catching sugars in the air,
Sent outside to stop my giggles,
Shamed, I chew my plaited hair,
Spiky word shape needs a locksmith
Suddenly decipher 'with'.

Brightly now the sun comes flooding,
Books, for me an open door,
Story time will be in my hands,
Won't be pleading any more,
Fist squeezed tightly in my pocket
This is brilliant, I can do it.

Canvas cot with musty smell
Hot veranda where we doze
Sandal sole of yellow dough
Flopping rubbery by my nose,
Sticky in my airtex vest
Joy still bubbling in my chest.

To Mrs Gaskell

Pig-tailed, Gran sat me up onto the slab
Of Mrs Pollitt's crowded corner shop
And while my granddad, muffler, cap and fag
Put on his bet with pals in the back yard,
I listened to a world you also knew,
A place of dirty streets that marked
The Whitsun white of my new shoes,
Where pride made netted windows shine
And Sarah Barton stoned my gran's front step
For decency, until the day she died.
I heard, 'they buried so-and-so last week',
Hushed whispers, how they 'took it all away'.
I felt the pain for him who'd 'got the sack',
The anger, he'd been 'quartered', the blank stare.

I met you first in Cranford, too genteel,
But yet a place where poverty could hide,
And later my same streets, a hundred years before,
With fears unchanged and smoke and fog and grime.
You took me to the houses of the 'posh',
The bosses, who'd employed my old great-gran
As 'knocker-up' to get folk to the mill
To do their shifts, attacked by noise and dust.
I met 'the other half', encountered good and bad,
The fighters and the crushed.
Your husband was the one to preach. You showed
The need for justice through the tales you told,
Shone light upon the only world I knew.
There was another way and I could take the road.

A Lovely Run

'Gertie', in reverse gear, groaning up the pass
we all stand anxious ready for the push,
everything gritted but the road,
or petrol-tensioned eyes seek fast rejected pumps
dejected by his 'cheaper back at home',
and our old motor never even slowed.

A photo brings back pressures of the day,
Mum perching prim beside the tin tray table,
me, shoulders sunk, gazing through a gate,
apart, and craving sympathy from cows,
teen-aged wretchedness a look would not convey.

And after, the nail-biting journey done,
oblivious, as he beamed in pride, would come,
'Now don't you think that was a lovely run?'

Picnic Place

They won't let me eat the picnic
Till we reach 'the place'
And so we traipse across the tablecloth
Well spotted in yellow on a ground of lettuce green,
To trudge along the scissor cut
Of crunching crisps nobbled with bun-like pebbles
And edged with coconut pyramids, strangely dyed.
Onwards we trail
Flanked by a mix of upturned yoghurt pots,
Where cheese-spiked hedgehogs scuttle
Through the near impenetrable slab cake,
The lemonade stream, hissing and fizzing beside.
We skirt the stacks of sausage rolls
Tramping among discarded cocktail sticks,
Trooping round the deep, still, setting-jelly pools
With banks of rough-heaped sandwich
Towards the open place with the smooth flat rock
Where, at last, the tallest giant candles
Catch light in the sun
To celebrate the edible feast to come.

Backward Look

There is a place,
I can't say where exactly,
somewhere south-bound on the M6,
where dozing eyes open and see
bricks,
heart-sinking, hideous bricks marching towards me,
bricks like the ones that walled in my childhood,
pushing against each other in terraced ranks,
drilled into straight streets of suburban semis,
uniformed bungalows in jarring red
or jaundiced orange, squadrons of
palatial new-build rabbit hutches
jostling for space, too close to collapse.

I want to u-turn, somersault,
wheel about and run, stagger, crawl
northwards, to where grey stone
sturdily defends green hills and woods,
individual, independent, firm
strongholds open to wind and sky where
long settled walls are no threat to the eye.

Return

This has been a forbidden place,
A place we could not go for such a time
Our thoughts about it were judged always wrong
So we were outcasts from a place we loved.
And then he died, your father,
He who was always right,
He who knew which hill we should have climbed,
He whose photos were set as a puzzle
We could not answer, weren't allowed to enjoy.

You'd showed me the lakes with such joy,
Taught me to feel the air outside my cities.
We'd stood in mist on the fell side,
Stared into dark mysterious tarns,
Grown closer to each other without words
Or description, till he analysed our walks
Out of existence, dowsing the pleasure.

And now he's gone, the funeral was today.
We travelled on north, to think by twilit lake
Unsure whether we were trespassing where
We should not be. May we now stand entranced
Among these silent darting bats and dare
To breathe this air again?

Love Poem

I woke when the night was still dark and I
Wanted to write you a love poem.
You lay there next to me so calm and I
Wanted to write you a love poem,
To bring back the way it began
And share how it steadily grew
And became
Mundane
An everyday, ordinary love,
Stronger than building blocks,
Warmer than woolly socks,
Boring but true.

But my heart couldn't tell my head
The right words,
And my head wouldn't guide my hand
The right way,
So I nudged you to cut off the snore
And went back to sleep,
But I
Wanted to write you a love poem.

No Magic

Our love did not grow in magic places
Where sunset wands touched silver
Sand and sea
And made a burning cauldron
Of the estuary mud.
Its colours were of oil on drizzled roads
Grey buildings and a smoky atmosphere
With gaudy hoardings
Advertising films.

Our love was not nurtured by the song of larks
Carolling spells over a hillside's green
Or curlews
Bubbling sorcery along
The tide-washed shore
Its music was the hiss of passing cars
Squealing brakes and yowling city cats
Sharp slamming doors and
Shared dripping taps.

And yet love worked its wizardry on charmless ground
Binding together two bemused and
Artless souls
And made a bond of iron
Marked with ring of gold.
And after this enchantment led we two
To share an alchemy of sights and sounds
Where miracles do not
Depend on magic.

Local Historian

Hunched over
His laptop
Whispering
To the dead
Eliza Stokes
Gabriel Tew
Where did they live?
What did they do?
Filling columns
Tap-tap, tap-tap
Mapping out
A village's
Darkened years.

Almost he sees
Their hopes, their fears,
Their goings on
Carrier, corn miller,
Stocking weaver,
Seamstress, servant,
Framework knitter,
Ag. Lab, Ag. Lab, Ag. Lab

At times seems more
At peace with dead
Than living souls
They don't question
Don't answer back
They simply keep
Their mystery
Hidden, illegible
In the dense wool skein
He's driven
To unwind.

Radiation

'It's cold again' she says. The doctor
Wrinkling walnut brow extends a hand
To examine the coolly impassive patient.
A sporadic outbreak of damp spots
Suggests the onset of fatal shivers.
The question mark on top of his head
Sinks to stir his 'Heat oppresséd brain'.
The Earth quakes, the seismograph
Forecasts an impending eruption.
The air whirls with a fury of gathering
Nuts, washers, valves and joints
The rusting harvest of forty years
None will be deemed worthy.

Kneeless in green jeans, he rides forth
To cunningly challenge the brown-coated dragon,
Smouldering keeper of coppery treasure
Seeking to answer the tangled riddle
Of which bit will fit,
Returns victorious pockets a-jingle
For nothing shrink-wrapped enters here.
Sinks to his knees before the blocked quarry
Lips sucked into a straight tight line
Sealed like a plastic freezer bag
And strikes to no avail.

His mate who's lost the vital spanner, wrench
Or what-not in the last engagement must
Seek the wide world over till it's found.
A final lunge 'And you, you brute'
Releases a 'slow black, crow black' sludge
And she the Sorcerer's Apprentice
Runs with bowl and bucket, basin and bottle
At his urgent, blue-tinged bidding till the slick
Is gone and Red Adair has capped the well.

The champion rising nobly from the knee
Demands reward, not medals, but
A steaming libation of freshly brewed tea.

Pause For Thought

Tall oak tree,
small girl
leans against the bark,
bright speck,
eyes shine out,
contrast to the dark.

What's she doing hovering there
foot propped up behind her?
Dreaming?
Wondering?
Making plans?
'Thinking' all she answers.

Small girl
gives a twirl,
runs off to find daddy.

Quest For Rhenigidale – After Keats

With crags above
Stride past the group
Of black-house circles
Camped beside the sea
To slog up the path
Six rising miles to
Isolated Rhenigidale.

Top the first ridge.
See zigzag ladder.
Dizzily descend
And know
That when
You reach
The bridge
You must
Climb up
 again.

Breath comes short
Though not for the man
Who carried the post
Here daily.
Scrabble the last bit.
See the spread
Of small stone houses
Your goal achieved.

But be mindful!
Look no further!
You might glimpse
The newly metalled road
That comes
The other way.

Stiomrabaigh

This is the site.
We can moor close by.
No use for fishing,
Fish-farming
Transport costs sky-high.
No road,
No competition.

Last tenants?
Gone abroad
Tierra del Fuego
Falklands
Ireland
Hudson Bay
Australia
Argentina
The U.S.A.
Did very well for themselves
So they say.

Nice little spot,
Romantic, remote
Neat country pad
For a man with a boat
And a good deep pocket.
Prices out here could
Go up like a rocket.
How does that light our fire?

Fire Place

You wouldn't find it unless you knew it was there.
The yomp over peaty tussocks gives no clue.
In truth there shouldn't be a way
Except by sea.

Silence so loud it fills your ears,
Stillness this summer day, belying
What the winter brings.
No air moves the loch nor the sea
Of grass around our feet. A plate of glass
Reveals the blotched and banded pebbles
Beyond the lace of beach.

Nothing grows now in the coffin lazy-beds,
But roots of houses push up firmly from the rocks
Marked out by strong, sharp nettle growth.
Stones of fallen walls, once battlements
Against invading wind and wave and rain,
Offer shelter to a sheep, who nibbles rowan
In the soot-stained hearth, where once
The peat fire never went out.
A lone blank window space stares coldly
At no-one, at emptiness
It was not made for this.
There is no answering gaze from friendly neighbour.

Wandering down to the waters edge, I find
A rust-blown poker half-buried in the sand.

Peaceful Orkney

The sea's the key to Orkney,
surrounding it, providing barrier and bridge,
link to Britain's furthest point, but moat too,
guarding still lochs and fields of sociable cows,
a quiet, deceiving air of calm and ease,
for this place has rarely tasted lasting peace.

It took a storm to show the village there
of Skara Brae, stone round houses linked for company
turning their backs on that same sea, the source
of food and trade and threats of enemy,
beds, dressers buried in deep sand, signs of a life
focussed on ceremonial stones and strife.

What ended that's unknown. For certain
it was gone before the Viking ships sailed in.
Men passing a cold winter in a tomb
scribed on the walls lewd messages in runes,
built, later, palaces of rich renaissance grace,
a place for scenes of feasting, drunkenness and butchery.

And to this day efficient roads bare witness
to preparations for world war, and sunken ships
lie sea-weed draped in chilly Scapa Flow,
where prisoners' loving labour built a church.
Still tourists tramp or flounce in flocks
to storm your sights and conquer your rough rocks.

Samarkov

There is no golden road to Samarkov,
It's dusty, rutted, pot-holed, rough and coarse.
There's cars with many horse-power, carts with one
Or donkeys, bullocks and a grazing, hobbled horse.

We'd finished our walk on flower-dressed paths
Through mountain meadows spreading high above
This run-down little town. Where had we come?
There could be nothing here, nothing to love.

Or remember. It was not photogenic
And yet the pictures stay, caught in my mind
The women washing carpets by the road,
Hosing the giggling children, faces lined.

But smiling, smiling like the man who calls,
'American? Bush. No, you English, Blair.'
and signs thumbs up as we move on towards
the mosque, the only noticeable landmark there,

But locked. We peer through chinks in boards to spy
Displays of floral plaster, painted bright,
Flowers beyond anything we'd seen above
Condemned to a darkness more harsh than night.

We searched but could not find a golden heart
In this poor town, a closed museum, soulless square
Was all, until the heap of peaches by the road
Bright fruit, bright face for sure we'd found our gold.

Cow Parsley

The lane has narrowed down again.
It happens this time every year,
when flowering keck sneaks into bloom,
is suddenly soap foam, frothy, white,
first bite for rabbits, delicate
snowflakes captured in a spiders web.

Anthriscus sylvestris its proper name,
but here's no prissy proper flower.
A vagabond straddles the path,
bursts out, crowding the roadside,
lurking in hedgerows, haunting ditches,
lair of jewelled beetle, grey moth, fly.

As children it called to us, there,
by the brook, longing to gather
jam-jar bunches for scullery sill.
Deeply we knew we must not touch.
Its feared name, May-mother-die,
warning in its musty, grassy smell.

So tell me, daughter, why it was
you picked it for your bridal day?
True it was May, cow parsley blooms
in May, would spring around your feet,
nestle with green herbs and roses
in your hands to make a country bunch.

Though old misgivings sought me out,
an undertone, a note of doubt,
for you, the sad old name unknown,
the brightness of the day undimmed
as you stepped out in silk and smiles
and on your dress embroidered Queen Anne's Lace.

Black Flower

As I crossed the road, it caught my eye,
lying with foul, mud-fringed edge,
a black flower, its stiff petals foot-crushed
between grimy gutter and kerb.

Time was when the whole world was seeking
treasure beyond priceless treasure,
not honeyed fruit nor healing herb,
but the elusive black tulip,
symbol of justice and right,
the source of vast fortunes lost and won,
and still the quest goes on,
Black Parrot, Black Hero, Queen of the Night,
each highlighted by darkness
but missing the impossible mark,
though dark, darker, incredibly dark.

But the colour I saw was true ink-black,
such black as was never earth-grown,
but woven in silk for adornment
now fallen, deemed totally valueless
along with its wearer, cheap,
not worth picking up.

Spring Paradox

Hedge sparrows strip leaves from the sage bush.
It is the time to build nests.
Tits halt in the bright amelanchier
En route to the box on the wall.
The robin waits in the magnolia.
The frost hasn't harmed it this year
All is an urgency of life that is and is to be.

Nature is not simple,
The orderliness of creation is not complete.
The frogspawn froze in the pond.
I found the empty blue shells of the blackbird eggs
Too soon upon the ground.
And now you lie, sweet child,
With father and mother
In a basket nest
Six inches of perfection held in love,
The start of life that has been and will not be.

Flake

I did not know
A snowflake could be so substantial.
So solid against my belly,
Belly of my child, your mother,
Hugging in joy, feeling so changed.
I did not know
An unborn child could be so present,
So clear seen only in a fuzzy scan.
Flake, child of snow, waving with the daffodils
Waving, please God, not drowning.

That was in that other world,
Of Easter resurrection,
Staring at ancient photos, wondering whose likeness
Flake would have.
And now I do not know,
Will there be a face to add to the archive?
Or simply an empty space
Where even this cold north wind
Could not prevent
A heartless melting.

Clare

Driving the dull, dank, gloomy lane,
peering through windscreen spotted with rain
hearing the slush of wheel on leaf
will sunk deep in lingering grief,
mist in the mind for what could not be,
curving beneath one more dripping tree
I see . . . .

'CLARE IS LUVLY' on the bridge
adorning the dark, smoke-blackened wall
in bright-white letters three feet tall,
painted by some love-drunk swain,
heedless of the threat of trains,
as into the night his love unfurled
sharing his joy with all the world,
and through the tunnel of the arch,
filtered by overhanging larch,
for me one beam of sunlight clear.

Clare

Misty day
Rain on the screen
Wet leaf and dripping tree
Peering ahead, I see
Letters shouting
Bright and white
'CLARE IS LUVLY'
On the blackened bridge
And the sun filters clear
Through the arch.

House Boasts Special Feature

This house boasts
Eight bright well-proportioned rooms
Immaculately presented
Vastly improved and extended
With a wealth of
Original charm
And character.

This house boasts
An excellent prime position
Popular village location
Benefiting from recent full
Modernisation
In generous
Well matured plot.

This babe, with
A wealth of original charm
And character, tipping the scale
At just eight pounds four ounces, joins
Her proud parents
Where, building-in
This brand new feature
This house boasts.

First Steps

After the painting by Vincent van Gogh

Out among vegetables he
spreads compost from the barrow
tending new-grown cabbage shoots.
Indoors I keep proud watch
over our own small seedling
clutching furniture legs,
an adventurous vine
clinging from point to point.

Across the earth he reaches,
spade abandoned at his feet,
willing her to embark
on a first solo voyage.
Balanced tightly in love
heart in mouth, breathless,
can I dare to launch her,
a small white-sailed craft
bobbing, babbling on green wavelets
making a wakeless path
to lurch into the harbour
of her smiling father's
outstretched, loving arms?

Sky Baby

Ellie's into sky-scapes,
Layer upon layer of horizontal impressions
As she stares intently upwards.
Sees stripes;
Stripes of stair and cot and ceiling beams
Then floating clouds, flapping birds
Washing slowly rotating
Snakes and parrots, giraffes and frogs
Circle and bob overhead
In a heavenly menagerie.
Trees startle into grins
And gazes of delight
Chasing each change of dappled light
And green upon green
Faces float up and down
Unfocussed reaching
Awakening smile.
Now she sky dives in her true element
Suspended high in her parent's hands
And I see her mirrored, the little Elf,
Grinning like some small Green Man
Among the trees reflected in the summer lake.

Pip or Acorn

Who called you Pip you firm infant oak?
An acorn grown strong in the womb,
Forcefully moving to your own plan,
Stubbornly turning your face from the scan,
Awkward, we might well have guessed you a man.
Yes, you were not apple but oak.

Why do we ask you to rest in our arms,
A soft, yielding bundle of flesh?
Dreamily flopping your head on a chest,
Compliantly sucking milk from the breast,
Falling asleep when we think it best.
No, you're not subject to our charms.

Then we'll rejoice in the person you've grown,
Firm from your roots in the earth,
Doggedly climbing the shoulder at hand,
Rigidly forcing down feet as you stand,
Determinedly shouting till we understand.
Yes, it's as an oak you'll be known.

Nicholas

I am a little afraid of you
Somewhere deep inside.
A little in awe though you
Have only six months to your name.
You lie quiet and calm,
No problem to your mother
And then you open your eyes and
Look into my soul.

It isn't that you're a solemn child
Your toothless old man grin
Shows dimples tied with invisible string
Like buttoning on our nursing chair
With cheerful ey-oh and gurgle
From the depths, you greet the world
Self-contained in serenity
And yet there's something else.

Born on All Saints Day
Your mother swore she'd cross her legs,
Till Halloween was over
She didn't want birthdays blighted
By plastic pumpkins, ghostly sheets,
Besoms and witches hats.
There's nothing sinister in your solemn look
Your knowing, been-here-before look.
Just a deep heart-searching peace.

Unnerved I view a thousand icons
In churches, monasteries, museums
The Christ-child looking like a little man
Shape, expression too mature for a baby
Arm outstretched in blessing
Standing wisely on his mother's knee
Just as you stand gazing outwards.
There's something about the eyes
I recognize. It frightens me.

Pippa

Philippa Mary Evelyn Sadler
Where are you hiding?
I'm coming to find you ready or not
I can't wait much longer, you're out of your cot.
You're walking, you're running, you're using your pot,
I can't spend for ever deciding.

There's no use to look back at me through your legs
With a grin that could cause global warming
Then rush off with Ellie to match plastic eggs
My proffered hug rigidly scorning.
You're a tease, you're a flirt, you are surely not shy.
You're a wanton with grandfathers, any old guy,
But for others the quizzical 'touch me not' warning.

You taught us the virtue of playing peep-boo
To de-stress a difficult meeting.
You taught cousin Freya the tummy display
As a form of juvenile greeting.
You taught two buns are better than one
When it comes to perfect party eating.
So don't pretend you can do nothing at all
Hiding your light is just cheating.

You are the one who's determined to win but
We know it won't work you'll always give in,
So don't go all coy there and lower your chin
One tickle will pop that balloon like a pin
Come out now I've broken your cover.

Adam

Someone is reaching his neck round the door
crawling at full speed on clattering floor.
Someone is one smile spread ear to ear
dimples in cheeks that just don't disappear.
Someone is swallowing food at a rate
no-one allowed to help empty his plate
if anyone tries to assist he'll create.
Someone is squealing to stand on his feet
such independence won't suffer defeat.
Someone's objecting to holding a hand
he'll walk on his own, all adult help banned.
Someone will climb every stair on his own
no interference, not now that he's grown.
Someone is singing a song to a star
loudly ensuring it travels that far
hurling and twirling his body around
rowing his boat . . .

Jigsaw World

How many pieces did it take
to make this world of ours
with skies and seas and elephants,
ducks, snails and cauliflowers?
God thought of all the pieces, chose
where each of them should go.
He made the plan to set it off
and make the picture grow.

How many people pieces live
here in this world of ours?
There's you and me and him and her,
we could count on for hours.
Ev'ry one has their own place,
right where they're supposed to be,
with things that they are clever at
and minds to make them free.

Lord thank You for our jigsaw world
with all its special parts,
and mostly for the big love piece
You put in all our hearts.
You've given us each our own shape,
and a way that we can shine,
so show us how to fit into
your marv'llous picture world.

For Clara

A shaft of winter-flowering sunlight
clear and bright
Clara Jasmin Woolf
blooms shining and new.

Treasure the earth's gifts
to match the purity of your name,
rich ground providing nourishment
for health and strength,
sparkling water to bring growth
sustain and cleanse,
sheltering cloud by day, a sky at night
jewelled with stars undimmed by light,
air, pollution free, energising life,
revealing a world unclouded by ugliness.

Let your mind and vision be as clear,
with hope and optimism and joy,
seeing a straight path ahead
unobstructed by murky prejudice,
guided by values to transparent goals
and pleasure in the way before you.
Loving and beloved, feel safe
in the protection of all who care for you
and venturing into the forest of your life
may the only woolves you meet
be familiar, friendly, family ones.

Learning Loss

Once I played with dad's handkerchief
Lowering it over the guard
Nearer and nearer the flames
Till, impossibly, it was gone.
Holidays, pantos, trips out
Pivoted over a ridge of time
Count up, count down
The sickening tilt to an
Anticipated ending.
The dahlias danced sambas
Till they hung in frost rags
Pink, red and gold
Instantly burned paper brown.
Friends go, places change,
We can't walk backwards to Christmas.
You wave goodbye to your birthday guests
And turning, with solemn, questioning eyes, say
'Granny my party's over now'.

Blossom Time

What a year it was for may blossom,
fluffy cloud banks tumbling into the canal,
stunningly soft and white above and below
the brown-green drifting water,
where sunlight sank, reflected, into blankets of flower.
Picking that delicate seed head,
you taught your sister to tell the time.

Another year, another day, your sons
walked by some other water
and finding dandelion clocks,
blew away time, till I was back
on that tow path, over the garden fence,
with you so carefully counting hours,
as your sister solemnly released
floating fairy parachutes
into the years still to come.

Safety First

Hit by an arrow to the heart, she freezes
'It's gone, my best tree!'
The willow chosen above other trees,
as dragon's den, fairy land or giant's castle,
as home or cave to hide and peep
or swing blissfully, like a leaf in the breeze
lies stacked in sections where once it stood
and a distraught five-year-old lies and weeps
a slender log in the summer grass,
not knowing or comprehending
the cause of her distress,
nor how something so strong and permanent
could ever be declared 'unsafe'.

Newton Suspension Bridge

A single rotting plank
Spanned the dribbling stream
So narrow it served its purpose
Spooking the cows
Who preferred the muddy paddle
To the greener grass.

A single ancient plank
Loved by the village kids
So low you could dabble your wellies
Slurping up frog spawn
Or other watery beasts
For a closer look.

A single crossing place
Unless you walked to the stones
Lone enough to stand and gaze
Ponder, dream, work things out
Without interruption
Without the need to explain.

The single plank has gone
The council called it a danger
Replaced it with concrete and bars
For climbing over,
A no-nonsense, functional bridge
Hardly used any more.

Memory Search

There's so much the folk here can dredge out
The tree that they hid in as kids,
The spring in the hedge where they came
With a yoke, the old chap who used
To be good for a joke, the ice in the lane
Where they slid.

A dig in the plot brings out more clues,
The details, it's true, are obscure.
What happened to shatter so much
Blue and white? When he broke his pipe
Was it anger or fright? And what was
That brass button for?

There are memory secrets hid deep here
That only research could reveal,
The plum tree that marks out where Biggin
Once stood, the barrier to plague
Where the fields always flood, and where did
The pilgrims once kneel?

The land still holds tight to its long closed book,
Some pages may never be turned
The mammoth once carved by the knife
Knapped from flint, the humps and the bumps in the field
That give hints at a whole way of life
Still unlearned.

Health or Safety?

The solid oak out in the park
has spent two hundred years of growth plotting
how to become a danger.
The softening planes at the road edge
have lately come under suspicion
of rotting with intent.
The fruiting horse-chestnut by the gate,
still tempting violence, is unjustly condemned.
In the playing field the yew, the last great poisoner
deserves dismemberment
and the willows by the river's safety rail
wail for those already executed.

Surprising how many people
have not been felled by falling trees
nor feared death on healthy walks
in fields and woods or urban parks,
are able to read warnings
                                         safely.

Helpful Warnings

If in life you want to be smart,
read the instructions before you start.
Ruins are ancient, the stone blocks may fall.
There's no further access where steps meet the wall.
Fence off the pond
lest the fishes abscond.
Watch that the chaffinch wipes its feet,
when landing on the bench to eat.
Do not proceed before boarding the boat,
you'll find that your car is unwilling to float.
Always keep a hold that's sound,
so children can't fall off the ground.
Ban the tooth-fairy just in case
her gift should tempt an exploratory taste.
When you have a plastic bag,
though you may find it quite a drag,
keep away from children.

An Inspector Calls

The day that the inspectors came
the world stood on its toes.
The twins cut down on the squabbling
and Umar blew his nose.
The paint stayed where appointed,
the water in the trough
and Miss got through the literacy bit
despite a nasty cough.
Liam greeted the visitor;
he put on a lovely show
and Miss just kept her fingers crossed
his temper wouldn't blow.
Reception was home to angels.
No-one put a foot wrong.
The tall man with the clip board
wouldn't be here for long.
He wandered round looking a bit lost
and then declared them all 'sweet'.
He wasn't used to such small folk
scrabbling under his feet.
He said he'd enjoyed his visit.
Miss breathed a sigh of relief,
the way that she'd held it together
was far beyond her belief.
He's going out through the door now
but Liam's made a new mate
'Why don't you come back after playtime?
We're doing PE, it's great.'

Fallen Tree

A surprise of sunlight in the kitchen
drew my attention to nothing, a space
checking the roll of features in the view
I registered an absence, double took,
but it was truly gone, that is to say
a half of it was missing, fallen down.
The tree whose leafless hand always spread
across the blue, the white, the shades of grey
providing visible perch for starlings,
owl, rook and crow was wounded beyond help.
There was no storm last night, no wind howling
no explanation for this sudden end.
It can't have fallen silently with such a bulk
and yet no sound was heard, there should have been
a fanfare, cannons or at least a bell's dull tolling
to mark with sadness the skeletal remains
the dry bones, not of one lost warrior,
a battalion of memories litters the grass,
of chases, picnics, quiet canoodlings
where now a single jagged finger nail
scratches across the surface of the sky.

Outlook

Gold gimped cushion clouds
scud at speed across cold blue
in the biting January wind.
Sheep huddle under bare trees
offering no shelter against shivers
but presenting a cobweb of branches
trapping rooks nest flies
to fascinate the eye.

Three pheasants parade in line,
ignoring the rabbit causing consternation
to a party of smaller birds, who rise
revealing black silhouettes
against the banks of cloud.

Below all is tired green
until a fleeting flash of sun spotlights
the digger's amber warning.

Sky Screen

Sodium blights the sky-screen
so bring on the sound-show now.
Romantic twitterings set the scene,
slap-stick clatter of pigeon wing,
eerie hoots of owl break silent hunt.
Strum the base beat of rotors
where high-note planes rise over
heavy hum of hurtling wheels.
Canadas carve a rasping groove
across the lurid stillness,
natural noise, un-natural.
Dull drubbing heart-throb thrum,
detecting eye-in-the-sky,
dragged from estate to motorway,
oppressive drone of modern urban dread.

Beneath the jaundiced glow, the digger,
delving deeper, row behind row,
unearths shards from times of un-tinted space
when there were stars on a moonlit silver screen.

Still Moment

A sheet of plate glass as far as the eye can see
not the usual picture under this still, grey sky
though not strange,
there's no movement in the dull water,
yet there's expectation.
Excalibur might at any moment, break the surface calm.

A wagtail, foraging amongst the fringing stones,
suddenly takes flight, slicing motionless air
to rest again, half hidden in the mud.
Diving grebes make no sound emerging
from the depths, only to dive again,
nor does the cormorant perched on a post
drying its wide-spread wings noiselessly,
whilst a flotilla of mallard, duck and ducklings,
sets forth on a stealthy sea voyage.
The hushed lake scene holds its breath.

The grating call of a crow breaks the silence.
A cyclist makes a parting
through cackling Canadas on the path.
The wake of a single boat unzips the surface of the water.
The air is suddenly swirling, whipping trees, shrubs, grass.
A circle grows from the first heavy raindrop

No Rainbow Required

Tapping on steadily
all the day
the night
the next day
nothing spectacular
only the steady rain
on the windows
down the chimney
soaking the ground
relentless
chilling the spine
making the door
impassable.

Out there
wet cows droop heads
the river gains speed
brims over banks
sneaks across fields
climbs tree trunks
makes pathways
pavements
village roads
impassable.

Now, silvered water
pale, pale sunlight
penetrates
we've only had
a gentle insight
into the world of
Noah, Manu,
Utnapishtim
without ark
dove or crow.
The day looks
passable.

Full Circle

The old house is empty after the flood.
We look at plaster-stripped walls
to see how they threw it together then,
un-keyed bricks, slate hearth, beams of wood
still bark-clad in places.

Who were those people then cast off the land,
building against the sun's time
not to lose a familiar place,
to find a task fit for strong hands
now that crops were gone?

The verge provided space on which to build
in the lane that led to the tip,
to set up a stocking weavers loom,
use sheep's wool from land they once tilled,
begin to live again.

And again the house looks to a new start,
carpet and curtains, fresh paint.
Sheep watch us begin to seek new rôles,
retired from past lives, the known parts
we can no longer play.

Angelo

By name he's Angelo and he hammers
like an angel, or rather
one of the cherubim, clothed in flame,
guardian of the small inferno of the forge
stooping over the anvil strong arm raised
to strike and shape the iron to his will.
He may well be the last
in the line of village smiths
beating their way back
to when records and maps first began here.
Nathaniel Hewitt, followed by wife
then sons, stoked the same fire,
breathed the same scorched air
still blackening bricks and beams
and belching out the smoke and smell of his work
to tempt you in
past, not the gates of Eden, but others as fair
of his own making, stacked against the walls,
for Sicilian-proud he'll not submit
his craftsman-farrier's skills for an English permit,
makes horse-shoes only to amuse,
employs his tongs in delicate twists
and twirls and garden curlicues.

I ask for a good strong dog-grate and then take in
the slow seraphic smile, the stretching of great hands
as he gets to grips with the new task,
measure, heat, beat, weld and bend with pliers
and when the winter logs blaze on the hearth
I glimpse a swarthy angel in the fire.

Pentecost

They gathered in a room
without comfort,
without your presence,
until the wind roared,
the flames licked
the words burst out
from their tongues
bringing the message of peace
in language fuelled
by Spirit, not spirits.

I knelt in front of the grate,
blew gently to fan
the spark to flames,
matches spreading fire
through the printed words
of a different story,
without comfort,
without your presence,
that many had read,
burning a message
fuelled by anger,
lighting broken wood
that never was a cross.

Broken Link

She spent the day writing her letters,
her links with her past life world wide,
alone now, she wasn't a fretter,
she'd friends but not here at her side.

To check that no shopping was needed,
she knocked at the neighbouring flat,
then set off to go to the post box
in her big coat and warm furry hat.

She thought about life back in Lagos,
the missionaries, pupils and friends,
the students who'd come here to visit,
the family news each one sends.

The light was beginning to fade now,
on her doorstep she pulled out the key,
then a mugger, who'd hidden in shadow,
grabbed her bag as she fell on her knee.

The money was not worth his effort
and somewhere the bag would be tossed,
along with her life-long address book,
with that a whole world would be lost.

Things

When they came she was watching the news
turned up loud so she could hear
for her eyes she'd switched off the light
no sense any danger was near.
Confused, she demanded they leave,
'I didn't invite you, please go!'
They left.
She wept,
'They've taken away all my things,
money and trinkets and rings,
all my little bits, my treasures,' she shook,
'I can't tell what else, I can't bear to look.'

But soon she was firmly raising her chin
'It's just things, only things that have gone.
I am not hurt and my friends are all here.
It is such a comfort to see you, my dear,
but for the memories, what they all meant,
it is only things, that's all.'

Lost Youth

He sits, no, slumps,
On the garden bench
Tears trickling slow
Caught with hasty
White handkerchief
Behind his specs
And he remembers

He recalls how
An eager lad
Keen to do his bit
Sailed into seas
More troubled than
He could dream of
The world ablaze
Before his eyes
No way to help
No hand could reach
His doubles falling
On the Dunkirk shore.

That summer day
He blessed his luck,
Returned, to lead
A useful life,
To do his best,
To serve his Lord.
He did not lie
Among the lost.
He went to sea
A cheerful boy
And came back home
Deformed into
A man.

Pilgrim's Left Boot

We've marched some miles
Right boot and me!
Me always first
Putting his foot in it.
We've covered some ground
One way and another,
Kicking up dust,
Leaving our tracks
As we carried him on
Regular and steady
With his shield of faith
His sword of the Spirit
And the rest.

Now they go in for
Your more modern boot
Lighter in the sole,
Ergonomically sound,
Flashing lights in the heel
For all I know.
Right boot and me
We sit on the shelf
With rows of others,
Not completely worn out,
Still useful, waiting for
The more discerning foot.
Army surplus.

Cup

This is the cup that holds the tea.
Of course, it's Fair Trade,
What else would it be?
With those poor folk all starving out there
It's the least I can do.

This is the cup that holds the gruel.
Of course, it's not much.
Sometimes it seems cruel but
With all these thousands of mouths to feed
It's the best we can do.

This is the hand that can't hold the cup.
It's simply too weak
And it falls in the muck.
What else would it do?

Baltic Impression

Far away there is a hill
not green, no space for grass,
but closely covered
in crucifixes, crosses
named and unnamed
where rosaries rattle
constantly in the wind;
a place eerie with memories,
built and crushed and built
again so the lost
would not be forgotten;
no red poppies welcome here.

Far away there is a city
where a green bridge
spans the dull river
and solid stone statues
mean so much less
than the green paint
restored nightly from
the communist red.

Under the city sickly
green paint covers
corridors and cells,
a tomb for suffering
and torture, where
for some the blood ran cold
and for others flowed.

Far away there is a forest
with carved monument
and sad Cyrillic inscription
marking the place
now lost in evergreens
dripping silent tears
where once the snow was red
with blood-stained graves
of those who did not
choose to dig.

Far away there is a land
of people down-trodden,
dejected, comfortless,
determined to survive,
where deeply-rooted oppression
allows the green shoots
of freedom to break only slowly
through the reddened earth.

Babel Babble

Lunch in the garden,
Peace and something sweet,
Jingle-jangle 'Talk to me!
Yes I can hear you'.
So can we!
'No, no, You're breaking up,
I'm losing you' There's sound
in plenty bouncing round,
but no communication.

Cliff path encounter,
Spanish, English, Dutch,
German, Polish, few words shared,
Oh, Babel, you've so much
To answer for!
Yet, pleasantries exchanged,
map information shown,
smiles easily atone
for lost communication.

Sea Trial

The aim, to beat, not see, the world,
The way, a course already planned
For endurance.
A woman sure that she could hold
A boat in hand.

Immense, majestic rolling waves
Made beauty's mark here for a while,
Hardly eternity,
The clock was more the heart of things,
Mile after mile.

A sleepless route through stress-filled seas
Wind-whipped, strenuous, then too slow
No track remains.
If there was much of joy in it
It didn't show.

There was, it's true, a love affair,
But not with bird or water beast,
Nothing that lived
The boat held close, as sister soul,
Sail, rigging, mast.

And was the purpose simply speed,
A desperate, life-ruling urge to win
A race, to scribe
A circle on earth's ocean skin?
In this, success.

Cross Currents

The perpetual turning of the clock
brings the tides flooding steadily
in and out,
washing down the drizzle-dirty street,
with its day's accumulation of litter,
in a lurid glow of sodium, head-lighted
by passing vans, cars and heavies.

Daily the town's run-down flotsam flows,
as the shift changes from day to night,
in and out.
Observe them interact or remain silent,
arrivals and departures,
as buses come and go, giving and taking
from the shop-fronted street.

The shop girl leans against the shelter
dying to get out of her shoes,
cool her aching feet, queues
next to the woman with weary eyes,
arms stretched by bulging plastic bags,
two in each hand,
each too tired to chance
more than a passing glance.

Jeans stretched on a straining rack of flesh,
bomber-jacketed arms wrapped around
each other, they climb heavily down,
and in an aura of chip fat, fags
and love,
are caught by the current and carried
cheerily towards MacDonald's,
calling ' 'night mate! ' as they steer
past the pirate in black shirt,
open to the waist, gold chain bling
at neck and wrist,
and, with practised swagger, he
forces a passage to the upstairs club,
now wafting down waves of music
in a heavy beat.

A young mother drifts to the queue,
ear fastened to a mobile phone,
seeming to talk to herself,
loudly, as she ignores the child
whining cold-handed in the push chair,
parked near the old man, who staggers,
back too erect, propped by walking stick,
fighting infirmity, fuelled by booze,
bound for a lonely room,
smoke-drowned lungs struggling
to pant painfully
in and out.

The bus arrives, disgorges
a gaggle of flirty loud gigglers,
star-spangled, bare midriffs,
tattooed shoulders and thighs,
impervious to cold and damp,
sailing forth for a girls night out
warmed by expectation and substances,
eyeing the passing gush
of emerging, scrubbed up, testosterone.

As the see-saw tips the rush of night
into the dark space left by the fading day,
their places are filled by others and
on and on
in and out,
until the clockwork runs down.

Dressing The Tree

Seeking tranquillity and Christmas calm
she gently hangs old treasures on the tree,
memories of places, people, times bring balm,
baubles, bright stars and angels flying free,
carved hearts, the Santa with the Chinese look,
Mum's crochet bell, the children's gold-sprayed cones,
the Swedish goat, the peacock, shepherd's crook,
creations made of straw in muted tones.

Pierced with a sword of thought, she changes mood,
hangs wreathes of sickness, tear-drops, empty plates,
shells, bombs and mines, homes lost in war or flood.
She craves the garland peace, the world awaits.
The child looks up with stars behind his eyes;
his granny listens to the news and sighs.

Celebration Scramble

Someone switched on the Yule buzz far too soon
The lights were twinkling gaily in the shops
Before we'd quite dismissed the summer moon

The shelves were all festooned with sparkly tops
Bright gift ideas assailed our shaded eyes
The sleigh bells soon took over from the pops

And food suggestions focussed on mince pies.
The pressure to count down the days was on
Long before hopes of angels in the skies

The Christmas Spirit, feeling put-upon
Rebels, stamps feet, refuses to be merry,
Declares the whole thing to be nothing but a con

Then turns to cakes and reaches down the sherry
For cakes and puddings never can be rushed
Goes out to check the holly is in berry

Cards, letters, parcels, keeps her secrets hushed,
Fights bravely through crowds of loud, boozy louts
It can't be done in time she's feeling pushed

Round about now come the old nagging doubts
Order the turkey, how big should it be?
Is it unreal to ask kids to eat sprouts

Just one more bauble, that's finished the tree
Candles and firelight add warmth and good cheer,
Last minute touches achieve 'Christmassy'.

There can be no doubt that to beat the reindeer
The whole thing must start a bit sooner next year!

Vermeer's Kitchen Maid

Calmly posed as though caught
Among your daily tasks
Silently, mindfully
Pouring milk from a jug
Frozen in time
You stand,
Bathed in the quiet glow
Of eternal, steady sunlight
Radiating peace from the casement
Onto the planned clutter
Of preparation below.
There surely must be bustle
In that house,
But you live the moment,
Held in lasting stillness,
An image fit for graving
On John Keats' Grecian Urn.

Soul Cake

It was there from the moment of waking,
not noticed the evening before,
a hungering, hankering feeling
which breakfast did nothing to cure.

I scouted around for ingredients.
The magical dish must be made,
to share satisfaction with others
before its rare flavour could fade.

The recipe books gave instructions,
they're fine if your purpose is clear.
Old photos brought back tasty memories
of picnics and parties and beer.

I went out and gazed at the garden
breathed something of green and fresh air,
then raised up my eye to look at the sky,
Heaven knows what I hoped to find there.

There were things that might introduce sweetness,
some fruity, some herby, some bland,
some that might add just the right touch of spice,
but none of it quite what I'd planned.

I tossed in the flavoursome morsels
with no sense the dish would come right
and whispered a few incantations.
The mixture must not be too light.

The end result verged on disaster
no way was it food for the soul,
then I tasted a small hint of something
as I gave up and scraped out the bowl.

Sowing The Seed

Work the soil to a fine tilth,
chopping lumps, removing stones and crocks.
With the trowel edge mark out the groove.
Half an inch deep is orthodox.
Now guide the floaty carrot seed,
tipping with care not to let it blow,
into the heart-line crossing the palm of
his hand, so many years ago.

Between the pens of old Ernie's hens
and Mr. Wetton's immaculate plot
regular deliberation broke out
about the benefits of emigration
Australia, the chosen destination,
where he swore the mare's-tails we dug
were tied off with a firm knot.

Mr. Wetton went, he stayed,
though only to suit her wish,
sublimating adventure in a neat row
of Alpine strawberries, sweet and pure,
but he never forgot.

Now two hands pull up the weeds,
burn the unforgiving twitch,
set out the cabbages, caulies and peas,
but whose?
For I see his hands, there, in mine,
as gently, I brush the new-sown line
 with soft soil, and water our shared row.

Squirrel in the manger

In the fruit cage on the plot grow strawberries,
barely showing above the leaves, hard and green as yet.
I wait in anticipation, watching for snails,
safely fenced against rabbits and neighbours pets,
such lust in my heart and taste buds.

Enter stage left, some fifty yards away,
an elegant ballet dancer in tu-tu of ruffled fur,
leaving her young safe in the sycamore drey,
a fetching disguise sufficient protection for her
to camouflage intended crime.

Precarious she steps out on the long high wire,
balanced by fan of tail, she teeters boldly on.
I'm half in love with the reckless grace of her
high above fennel, rosemary and tarragon,
the carrots, caulies and bean poles.

Twice and again she loops the loop in her passage
clinging tenaciously with grasping finger and toe.
A silver grey current flows in waves through the cable
and plunges resolute to the safety net below,
the vault between her and the prize.

Returning later, I discover the Topkapi hole
determinedly gnawed by teeth intent on frugivorous crime,
below, a litter of berries scattered in wild rage,
rejected as she snipped them, one at a time.
If she can't eat them nor shall I.

Snail Trail

The enemy is there I see
Galloping up my apple tree,
He's thoroughly holed my new potatoes
Made neatest doors in my tomatoes
And now he's racing for the beans
He's reached the plot and now he means
To scale them.

You'd wonder how he moves so fast
When I pursue I roll in last
He's suitably dressed up for the chase
In stripy helmet over blank face
What can I do to drive him hence?
Ah, now he's heading for the fence
With vigour.

He's made it out into the lane
He's aided there by last night's rain
He doesn't pause to taste a daisy
He doesn't want to appear lazy
But here comes something moving faster
I think at last he's met his master
Big tractor.

Celebration Shelf

First spring's a problem, steals my time away
Wet earth to dig, so many beds to sow
Each muscle aches before the end of day
The weather's wrong to make the seedlings grow.

Then summer is a pain with swarms of weeds
And lack of wet that isn't from a hose
Next autumn looms, I turn from other needs
To endless picking as a whirlwind blows.

Now winter's here at last, the toil is over
All's frozen, chutneyed, jammed, stored safe from harm.
New catalogues display beguiling covers.
There's rain and snow and hail but I am warm.

So, smugly, to congratulate myself,
I count the rows of jars upon the shelf.

Un-Summer Day

There's a smell tells it's Autumn,
so, though the world outside the door today
has droop and mizzling dampness hanging over it,
that season isn't here,
there is no Autumn smell.
Spring too is easily discernable by nose
only a few steps down the path.
It isn't related to any specific element,
but it's there, its own self,
waking delight, making us look
for fresh bursts of new green,
putting a spring into the step.
Winter's scents are indoor, man-made,
wood fire, cocoa, Christmas cooking.
Outside sharp frost nips the nose,
other senses bring recognition,
touch and sight of shrivelled endings.
A nasal way to register Summer's arrival?
Mown grass perhaps, a fix of lupin,
honeysuckle, clover, old shrub rose,
a mix of occasional perfumes,
not guaranteed but hoped for.
Surely the misery of this scentless, downcast day
will never be what we with sighing
label Summer.

The Winter Is Past?

All last week the air seemed much warmer.
You could feel some slight heat from the sun.
Now looking out through the window
the view through the glass signals cold.

The field is disguised by deep snowfall.
The green is quite hidden from sight.
The pond has a rough dimpled ice sheet,
 impenetrably covering life.

Bare branches are holding slim white snakes,
dark tree trunks are ivory streaked,
whilst crystalline icicles hang sharply down and
rare brown leaves are coated in frost.

A trellis disfigured by footprints
makes clear the paved pattern beneath.
There's a soufflé in each of the plant pots.
A counterpane covers the wall.

Deep Winter seems with us for ever,
the time of snow frozen in place.

Yet a bright pair of persistent blue-tits
inspect the nest-box on the house
and a single clump of green sword tips
points skywards, piercing the crust,
towards the approaching Spring.

Change

The neat t-strap sandal on that young girl's foot
is the one I still wear in my head.
I can still ride a bike, roller skate and climb trees
'in my dreams', as observers may say,
in my eternal internal youth.

So why does my body refuse to agree
with these facts that my mind doesn't doubt?
The traitor knees tremble, the weak muscles fail
the firm balance deserts at my call.
External reflections tell lies.

Does the cat know it can't catch the mouse any more?
Does the mouse find it safer to hide?
The birds, bees and fish have no knowledge of change
but awareness is forced on my mind
in an elegant new summer hat.

One Day

One day
I'll shilly-shally in the shade
of a Caribbean shore,
one day
I'll dance to an African beat
in Africa
one day
I'll tremble in a temple
at the beautiful bizarre,
breath the brightness
of a northern midnight sun,
see the sky above Himalaya.

Young, you wisely did your thing
rainforest,
barrier reef,
the colours of the desert,
for us
no time,
no money
and endless self-imposed responsibility,
but one day....

A man with a medical file
and a rueful, hopeful smile
may well have just cancelled
one day.

The Last Dance

Laughter bowls down the lane to meet us
from the bride in medieval purple,
with cherry picking out the dreadlocks
and the train that trails in the stack yard mud.

Eighteen pretty-maids, dressed in their best,
giggle, as the 'best son' makes his six year old speech,
and she rushes to her newly wedded husband
with the thank you kiss he receives with suited solemn pride.

Later we watch as stripped of long robes
she whirls in wild response to joyful jazz
and a swish of swallows skims the swaying heads,
between the tented shelters of her guests.

Gyrating shapes build a glad tableau.
Hands and feet respond to the sounding beat.
Our wistful eyes meet, as I wonder
'Is this the last dance you'll save for me?'

Uphill Push

With Sisyphus it was a rock,
smooth, rounded, unresisting
to the downward pull of gravity,
never ending struggle to come
to rest, punishment complete,
on the mountain peak.

My labour to herd the tough-shelled crab,
turn its endless side-stepping forward,
halt its onward spread, make it meek.
Still, knowing there is no end to the task,
knowing we cannot let the creature bask,
I, like Sisyphus can only push on.

The Blossoming of a Bosom

There was a time, some time ago,
When I had bosoms, you should know
But cancer came, as cancer can
We didn't let it win, but man,
It robbed me of a bosom!

Years went by with 'flexible friend',
Pink prosthesis pride could lend
Small blancmange without a dish
Might just float off like jellyfish
It wasn't exactly a bosom!

No-one was cruel, no-one slighted,
Once in clothes appearance righted
There was no cause to take a rise
Till I saw pity in someone's eyes
Poor thing! She's lost a bosom.

Super docs took note of my plight
"Reconstruction will help with the fight".
Word, in time, led onto deed,
Cuts, then drains felt like a lead,
But worth it for a bosom!

Now it's done, or nearly so,
Dreams of home, eager to go,
Not from hands clever and kind
Just let's get this experience behind,
And keep the brand new bosom!

No more envying figures pert!
No more wondering which tee shirt!
No more sending for bras with pocket,
Somewhere to dangle a pretty locket
Oh! thank you for my bosom!

Upon Experiencing Male Hormones

A man's a creature born to doze
To light a fire and warm his toes,
Or nose, as fits the occasion.
His mind will never butterfly.
It charges on, a hunt in full cry
Of one objective at a time.
A single thought is always prime,
If he can remember.

A man's a being made for sleep.
He'll never hear the timer's bleep,
Or know why first he set it.
He'll nestle down behind a screen,
Newspaper, book or magazine,
A shape rectangular or square.
He won't be seeing what is there.
The snore betrays him.

A man's a mortal who needs a nap.
He simply can't help being a chap.
It's in his hormones.
You may well wonder why I believe this,
What observation's behind this thesis.
It isn't prejudice aimed to mislead,
Nor bias from a feminist creed,
I know, I've tried some.

Scan

Sliding inward
That's it starting
Ching ching
Ching ching
Air sound roaring
Rats are gnawing
In my stomach now
On and on it's
Unremitting
Ching ching
Ching ching
Suddenly it's gone.

Here's the hammer
Tang tang
Tang tang
Mustn't move
In my tube
Clang clang
Bang bang
On my iron tomb.

Drum and drill
Must keep still
Hypnotising
Panic rising
Concentrate
On breathing.

Shush shush
Shush shush
Shush clang shush
Balance
On a fence post
Spine heat
Heart beat
Will not squeeze
The buzzer.

Ching ching
Clash bash
Hitting hitting
Hitting hitting
Head beneath
The earphones
Splitting
Nerves vibrate
Ching ching
Loose all weight
Ching ching
Levitate
Ching ching.

Slowing down
Ching ching
More air sound
Ching ching
Sliding now
Sink to ground
Out into the open.

Colour Therapy

Tether me now if
you can find the life roots
under the skin bark.
Warm, tap and warn me
of sharpness to come,
flowing weirdly, chemically
alien.
Pump in the meths-purple,
no heather hills, flowers and
Scottish sunset skies.
Pump in the slime green-yellow
of drying, dying, grass.
It does not hold soft sand
or summer sunshine days.
Drip, drip from the shrouded bag
the blue, blue that calls
to the mind it closes down
of periwinkle cloudlessness and
sea without horizon, cool space,
a blue-note route to freedom
through lethargy's yawning waters.
Tether me deep and set me
free from the crevice-lurking crab.

Eyes

Looking at my fellows
I see eyes full of anxiety
shrinking from the scene,
I see eyes full of sorrow
at what may now be lost,
I see eyes full of fear
of needles, hurts and pain,
I see eyes full of uncertainty
knowing and not knowing,
I see eyes staring outwards
wondering about the future,
I see eyes full of determination
to beat what may come next,
I see eyes full of hope
that the future will be brighter,
I see eyes full of joy
at good news given,
I see eyes in the mirror
looking back at me,
my eyes,
knowing and showing all this.

Hospital Love Seen

Nursing Staff

Enter the brisk field of battle,
Send in the spies, vital signs.
Roll in the weapons
drug, drip and blood.
Lob in the care beam.
Retire!

Mother

She's sorted the kitchen and bathroom,
the jumble kept under the stair,
she's plans for the carpets and curtains,
her crochet waits there on the chair.
The seeds for next season decided,
she's dealt with the veg in the shed,
but her domed head is stuck on the pillow,
if she could just get out of bed.
This here is no lady defeated,
when the girls come she'll pull out the grin,
discuss magazines, films and soap-stars,
it's not time to toss the towel in.

Orderly

Dreamy-methodic his mop sweeps the floor,
Cornelius, swept from his land,
dignified, down-cast eyes craving a smile,
yearning for something to end this exile,
bring back home faces and hands.

Friends

We're sorry we're late, couldn't find you,
the parking, the entrance, the ward.
They hug, hold her hand, assess, smiling,
dole out the sweets that she'll hoard,
enquire about treatment and comfort,
'Oh no, I'm not lonely', she quips,
'I dance to the loo down the way there,
but my partner's a bit of a drip.'
Her priest popped in earlier this morning,
beamed bonhomie, blessing benign,
They'll care for the house, garden, milkman,

make sure that her cat doesn't pine.
She chuckles and chats to convince them
and they won't find the fear that's inside.

Husband

More precious than rubies is she
who sips water from the syringe
he trembling calm holds to her lips
dropping in love, drip by slow drip.

The Nurse

Waits till the rush is all over,
looks in to see what she'll find,
sits in the gloom of the half-dark
seeing through clouds in the mind,
sensing there's nothing to say,
doesn't attempt being kind,
practically offers a fresh cup of tea
and knowingly touches the hand.

The Weed of Hope

The weed of hope
Is convolvulus twined round my heart,
Is ground elder threading its way through my day
Sending up suckers in every normal action,
Is thistle and nettle goading with pricks and hurts
That will not let acceptance come,
Is the deep dark rooted mare's tail
That goes down into the soul.

Where is the solution
That will end my digging and delving and disturbance of the ground?
Shall I paint the leaves with the poison of despair?
Shall I attack with the flame thrower of anger?
Shall I pray for a numbing frost to hold hope back?
Only an unwanted death can end this hope
Kill out this most tenacious weed, making space
To allow the shoots of peace a place to grow.

Picturing The Past

Show me!
I do remember this!
We had some lovely days there, but
when was it, now?
Where was it we went?
Who came with us that day?
How did we get there, did you say?
What was it we specially wanted to see?
Which of us took this picture, then, hey?
And why, won't you please tell me,
if it's all so clear in my mind,
can't I, myself, unaided find
the answers to these questions?

Hide And Seek

She'll never find a joker like me.
There are such good hiding places.
She can shake her head as much as she likes.
She won't dislodge me.
Of course, sometime later on,
when she's given up the hunt,
I'll pop out, wave myself about,
blatantly, just to tease.
It's a game that gives me
such a kick.

It panicked her most in lectures,
when she knew she needed me.
I backed away further and further
with her in pursuit, till she gave up,
circling round me, knowing that front limb,
I left casually peeping out, was mine,
but only a sign, just enough to torment.
In conversation, she can cope.
I haven't a hope of winning.
They all know the game too well
and simply end up grinning.
Only her daughters begin to worry.
They aren't in any hurry to join in.

You wonder where I hide?
Well I am always to be found
in the thick, heavy book,
though you need to know
what you're looking for in the crowd.
Writing, she'd be proud to find me there.
The thin book could help
if I'd given her the 'sounds like' clue.
For her the best is the middling one.
She's usually got the gist
of what it's all about.
That book could lead her straight to me,
if I don't look out.

It isn't usually a game for the young.
You mature into it over years.
No point in wasting tears.
Simply wait for your elusive partner.
Sit back and think of ...
What was it now?

Sans Not Quite Everything

Her photo smiles down from the wall there
A young woman lit up by love
That image that she's long forgotten
With sepia power still to move.

She doesn't know now who her own are,
She can't either stand or sit up,
Her camera smile is long switched off,
Someone must balance her cup.

We wait and we wonder 'What's it for?'
This life that seems shrunken past hope
But her husband still faithfully visits
He always was one to cope.

He sits at her side as the days pass
No matter what pain it may cost
Then she clasps his old hand in her own two
And makes sure that not everything's lost.

Hands that hold

Hand reaching out
Not the remembered hand
Leading this child along
Sea shores, country lanes, shopping streets
Matching companionable stroll
To my tethered skip

Hands pulling on
Children racing down a slope too steep
Tipping wildly in the grass
Piled together giggling mad
Galumphing wellies
In confident march

Hand grasping now
Soft claw, almost cruelly strong
Dragging upon the one
Reversing before the slipper
Slithering feet
Of her supported walk

Hand clinging tight
Young child swinging soft, new made
Tiptoe-teetering in spurts
Urgent to grab a passing cat
Emerging steps
Join future to present and past.

Life Sentence

Death took you slowly
'Til you were finally gone
Lost over the years by a steady slippage,
Which denied grieving, seemingly for ever,
Or made it a permanent state.
Death snook in as depression
Kidnapper, tying you lifeless
In a chair, mourning the world,
Poisoner putting an end to joy,
Counterfeiter forging a face for visitors.
Death tip-toed about you,
Stealing your mind in piecemeal dementia,
Substituting frustration, frenzy, fierce anger.
Death came last as the gentle warden disease
Discharging you from the sentence that was life.

Saying Goodbye

She's saying goodbye.
She would never admit it
But it's happening anyway,
Visits to places long-loved,
Significant, symbolic
Of where she will not go again,
Or ever go now,
Repetition of children's parties
A generation on, home-made cards,
Crocodile cake, red rabbit jelly and fun.
She's touring the cottage garden
To find the memory plants
Given by this one and that one
On this or that occasion.
She's drinking in beautiful things,
Feeding a need.
Soon I shall stand close beside her
Watching the bonfire glow fade
No voiced words passing between us
To show its another goodbye.

Bus

The bus sets off from 'the Maternity'.
We stand and wait like packets on a shelf.
This bus pauses passing Toys 'R' Us
Leaving slow oil snail trails
Through changing traffic lights.
We stamp our frozen feet
Like soldiers keeping in step.
This bus dances past the Locarno, next stop
The park with it's seductive shadows.
We huddle together like sheep in the rain.
This bus rumbles round the estate
Where tired terraces grow in the litter beds
And kids need leads to keep them safe.
We shudder and moan like wind in the chimneys
And we wait,
               until,

'It's here'. The cavalry charge begins
Though the bus is headed for 'the Infirmary'
The cemetery, the life beyond.

This bus has a clock ticking on the front
But we have queued and we will get on.

Door To Change

'No Love! He's not there any more,'
They say as my three year old hand
Reaches for the knob.
Same old knob, bashed and polished
By hands, including mine,
Same old door, grained in the fashion of the day,
On top of the Victorian panels,
Door that once led to the farmhouse parlour
Leading to the parlour still
But now in a house surrounded by many.
Lowry streets, where once were fields.
The only field left given over to Rugby.
All is change!

And here is change too.
No more my cobbler granddad
Coughing and wheezing in his bed beyond the door.
The ebony elephant still stands
Beneath the table full of coloured bottles.
The itchy horse-hair sofa
And three brass monkeys,
See-no-evil and friends,
Are in their usual places.
But he is gone, and gone completely.
No face remains,
Only a big black boot
And the door to an empty room.

Where Were You?

Dressed in blue, your favourite colour,
An alien lay in a box in the room where
They ushered me to say goodbye,
Like some stupid Christmas doll
And I could hear you say
'It hasn't got a very pretty face'.
I looked for you, but you weren't there.
How could you be, your non-conformist self,
Guarded by Catholic Madonnas and cherubs
Despised candles at your head and feet?
I placed a dutiful kiss on the cold, cold plastic
That never was you and directed tears of anger
To wherever you might be.

Limbo

They're waiting for the dance.
As far as can be fathomed
Augustine played the tune,
So afraid himself of dancing the Primrose Path
'Give me chastity – but not yet'
Cheerlessly condemning each who could not
Pass the baptismal bar, righteous heathen,
Babe or soul unknown, to a fate
Worse after death.
No mother, father, secular or holy,
Could face the thought of burning babes
Or a Hell paved with infant skulls,
Without intentions.
Pious pity granted then a holding bay,
Outside the boundary wall of hallowed deaths,
Caught between joy and sorrow in
Perpetual separation,
Cause of Tess's bungled baptism,
Not much of a consolation.

So praise the papal broom that sweeps
The place clear, declares a God's love
Not less than human,
Bending backward to make an open space
And looking upward
Let the dancing begin.

Free Spirit

I look and I see
What you see.
Bone en-masse, teeth, eye spaces
A nonsensical jumbled heap
Of skulls, including mine.
It was mine,
But look closer.
There's no-one there
All you really see is vacancy,
Used-to-be people,
Used to be trapped in life,
Free now from all that load.
Free from need to, have to
Free from should do, won't you?
Time, pain, mental strain,
Free from body, free
From binding memory.
Separated bones,
Stored with no meaningful stones,
Keep them if you will,
To me it's immaterial.

Newbold-on-Avon Remembrance

Frost gives a muted greying sadness
broken by poppies challenging mourning
with their incandescent brightness.
Below the war memorial
we stand foot-frozen, waiting, cold
on the long straight path that leads
to another world, another time,
suffering the gentle aerial bombardment
of leaves as they fall, white and stiffened,
heavy with frost.

What salt-of-the-earth mothers still grieve for their sons?
Impossible to countenance,
my own children, so young, shivering there,
surrounded by the stones of the comfortable, natural dead.
Uniformed children uncomprehending
follow the straight shoulders of Fred,
erect for all his age, proudly leading
the dwindling few carrying
memory, flag and dignity into a new day,
'Remember', written on each furrowed face,
whilst the young bugler, hearing scribed names
of village families still known, remembering nothing,
reverently sounds out the Reveille
awakening us to the life of which
they should be part.

The Burial Track To Luskentyre

We start amongst the sharp rocks of the east
The land of banishment, when sheep meant more than men,
And head for Luskentyre, spared for the dead,
By way of the burial track, a boggy trench
Sunk between grey gneiss blocks, blocking all view
Dark, dank, the rock-strewn, trodden way unsure
Marked best by stone stacked cairns, devised to rest
Coffins, borne sturdily, lovingly west.

Our feet, plunged deep, engulfed in brackish peat,
Heavily tread this slow, high way of death
Till we break out and from the final ridge
Beyond us see an endless field of blue
With grazing, white, ethereal flocks
In pastures where there are no fearful rocks.

Ring Of Brodgar

We visit the stones to commune
With the spirits of the long dead,
And find they are fled?
Gone before the approaching feet
Of the spirits of the living
Carried here in coach loads.
Slow Buddhist circumambulation
Of the cinematographic kind
Hold in mind not Buddha, dharma, sangha
But see it, do it, get the information
And then pass on.

We protest at this intrusion,
This corruption of intended holy stillness,
But wasn't it very like this
On days of festival, of celebration,
When ancient ones gathered in crowds
Moving in time with rhythms sounding
As strident as the motor horns
That call these tourists back
To bustling life?

Candle

One lone candle
Speaks of enlightenment
Peace, joy, a vigil,
The very presence of God.
Some place two together
The special light of festival
Celebrating the birth of earth
And light itself
Or
Signifying the symmetry of
Father and Son
Earth and Heaven
Life and hereafter.
Then gather together many,
Offered in petition,
Pleading for forgiveness,
Remembering,
Pouring out thanks
Or
Shining brightly to welcome
The footsteps of a deity,
The victory of deep good,
A dazzlement of lights together.

Yet each candle glows with single purpose
A lone light
Of symbol, pilgrimage or prayer,
Mirrored in the soul
Of someone, breathing there.

Index and notes

18.   No Magic

19.   Local Historian – Meg often complained that Noel spent more
        time with the former residents of Newton than he did with
        her. Noel is familiar with the names and occupations of many
        of those interred at Clifton-upon-Dunsmore Cemetery and he
        feels himself to be amongst friends when he visits Meg's grave.

20.   Radiation – Noel was the plumber in the Barratt house. As in
        this description of him mending a radiator the air was often
        blue, but he always had the right bit somewhere in the garage.

21.   Pause for Thought – We know that 'daddy' in this poem is Noel
        but couldn't tell you whether the small girl was Ruth or Kate.

22.   Quest for Rhenigidale – Like the villages of 'Stiomrabaigh' and
        Lemreway ('Fire Place'), Rhenigidale is a Hebridean village
        accessible only on foot or by sea. At least it was when we first
        walked there, but then they built the new road...

23.   Stiomrabaigh

24.   Fire Place

25.   Peaceful Orkney

26.   Samarkov – Samarkov is a small village in Bulgaria. Noel and
        Meg visited to see its monastery.

27.   Cow Parsley – Ruth's wedding gown embroidered with herbs
        was made by Meg, and Ruth included cow parsley in her bridal
        bouquet.

28.   Black Flower

29.   Spring Paradox – The 'sweet child' was Meg's first grandchild,
        Christian David Glyn Williams, born to Ruth and Owen at only
        16 weeks gestation. It was Meg's outpouring of emotion at the
        loss of Christian, that marked the beginning of her poetry in
        earnest.

30.   Flake – Christian David Glyn Williams, known in the womb as
        Flake.

31.   Clare – Meg wrote two versions of this poem – the first instinctive, the second following discussion with Don Barnard, who lead the poetry group at Percival Guild House in Rugby and whose opinion Meg valued and respected.

32.   House Boasts Special Feature – Surprisingly Meg did not write this poem about any particular child. It was inspired by the property section of the local newspaper.

33.   First Steps – After the painting of the same title by Vincent Van Gogh (oil on canvas 1890).

34.   Sky Baby – Eleanor Louise Sadler, born 7th May 2002, first daughter of Kate and Antony.

35.   Pip or Acorn – Gregory Huw Glyn Williams, born 13th October 2002, elder son of Ruth and Owen. He was known as 'Pip' whilst in the womb.

36.   Nicholas – Nicholas Robert Glyn Williams, born 1st November 2004, younger son of Ruth and Owen.

37.   Pippa – Philippa Mary Evelyn Sadler, born 4th December 2004, second child of Kate and Antony.

38.   Adam – Adam Daniel Sadler, born 27th September 2007, youngest child of Kate and Antony. Meg was still working to complete this poem when she died. This is the most recent version from her note book.

39.   Jigsaw World – This hymn was written by Meg for the Christening of her youngest grandson. It is in Double Common Metre: we chose the tune 'Kingsfold' for the Christening.

40.   For Clara – Written for Clara Jasmin Woolf, a child of friends, for her naming ceremony.

41.   Learning Loss – This poem was inspired by a word from Gregory to his Granny on the occasion of his 4th birthday.

42.   Blossom Time – Ruth and Kate grew up in a home close to the canal in Newbold on Avon.

43.   Safety First – The tree in question was a willow in the rose garden at Nostell Priory, the child was Ellie Sadler.

60.   Pilgrim's Left Boot

61.   Cup

62.   Baltic Impression

64.   Babel Babble

65.   Sea Trial – Meg struggled to comprehend what gave Ellen MacArthur her urge to circumnavigate the world. She acknowledged her bravery but could not see the necessity for the challenge.

66.   Cross Currents

68.   Dressing the Tree

69.   Celebration Scramble

70.   Vermeer The Milkmaid painted c. 1658-60

71.   Soul Cake

72.   Sowing the Seed – The 'he' in this poem is Meg's father, Arthur, the 'her' is his wife, Hilda.

73.   Squirrel in the Manger

74.   Snail Trail

75.   Celebration Shelf

76.   Un-Summer Day

77.   The Winter is Past

78.   Change

79.   One Day – We would like to dedicate this poem to Professor Robert Grieve, the 'man with the medical file', who treated Meg at University Hospital Coventry and Warwickshire, until her death some 25 years later. Kate can't believe he still looks so young!

80.   The Last Dance – Meg and Noel joined their young neighbours for the wedding reception in the farm yard on Little London Lane in 2008.

81. Uphill Push – Those familiar with Greek Mythology will recognise Sisyphus whose punishment was to roll a huge stone up a hill to the top. As it constantly rolled down again just as it reached the summit, his task was everlasting. Meg compares this to her 25 year toil against cancer.

82. The Blossoming of a Bosom

83. Upon Experiencing Male Hormones – Some of Meg's treatment was based upon male hormones – she was glad of the insight into Noel's world.

84. Scan – MRI equipment is noisy and sometimes overwhelming.

86. Colour Therapy – Meg received a number of courses of chemotherapy, the chemicals used being an array of bright colours. Her use of the imagery of the crab representing her cancer appears in this and a number of her other poems.

87. Eyes

88. Hospital Love Seen

90. The Weed of Hope

91. Picturing the Past

92. Hide and Seek

94. Sans Not Quite Everything – Meg's Mother, Hilda Buckley, suffered from Alzheimer's Disease. Meg wrote this, 'Hands that Hold' and 'Life Sentence' trying to come to terms with this sad illness.

95. Hands that Hold

96. Life Sentence

97. Saying Goodbye – Meg and Elizabeth Langley made a long lasting friendship after living as close neighbours in Newbold. Sadly, Liz died of cancer in August 2008. Meg and Liz now lie side by side in Clifton-Upon-Dunsmore cemetery.

98. Bus

99. Door To Change

100.   Where Were You – Meg's experience of seeing her mother laid out was not a good one. Noel, Ruth and Kate found their experience of saying goodbye to Meg much more positive.

101.   Limbo

102.   Free Spirit – The Stone Age 'Tomb of the Eagles' is in the Orkney Islands. The skulls were deliberately separated from the other bones within the tomb.

103.   Newbold on Avon Remembrance – Ruth and Kate paraded as guides on Remembrance Sunday each year.

104.   The Burial Track to Luskentyre – The land on the eastern side of the Isle of Harris is too rocky to bury a coffin. Instead the dead would be carried across the burial track to the deeper ground on the western side of the island.

105.   Ring of Brodgar - A ring of standing stones on Orkney

106.   Candle

For Meg – The short poem on the back cover, written just after Meg's death, seems to sum up her poetry. Thank you Glyn for allowing us to reproduce it here.